Joy, pain, and everything

Inbetween

Joy, pain, and everything

You loved me, you lost me

But look what you taught me

I should hate you but I can't

My heart hurts its true

But not as much as it did while with you

I was broken before you

Thought you would fix it

But it's my job now

To just keep on living

Hate

Is it the absence of love

Or its melancholy twin

Is it obsession, desire

Or simply a sin

Does it justify revenge

Or tear a life apart

Is it always hiding

Deep down in your heart

Are people born with it

Like a malignant disease

Or is it created when love

Starts to cease

I don't understand it

I know no one does

But we still try to fight it

Simply because

We know a life with it

Isn't worth living

But a life without it

Is only just beginning

I look at her

She's beautiful

She looks like she

deserves the world

I look at him

He doesn't see the

Beauty right in front of him

If he breaks her heart

He won't even care

It'll be like she was never there

But worst of all

If he hurts her

It'll make me happy

But who's to know

Maybe he'll break me too

Look how close we were once

And now all that's left are memories

I don't know what I did

that led you to hate me

I'll look back once more

At the good times

But then i'll let them go

For what's the point of memories

If all the good ones lose their glow

You've probably forgotten

The way I made you feel

But once upon a time

We thought our love was real

Maybe we were younger then

And didn't understand

There's more to love than just

Holding someone's hand

But darling I forgive you

There's nothing left to say

And i'll bid you farewell

As I finally walk away

Burning flame to dying ember

A mild spring to frigid winter

All good things must come to an end

But I didn't believe that then

I took my time

but I blew my shot

At least it wasn't all for naught

I learned my lesson

And now I know

Some things are better

If you let them go

No strings attached doesn't negate the emotions

Without a relationship hearts can still be broken

Culture will tell you it's normal not to feel

But don't buy the lie

The devastation is real

Despite all the labels all the strings are still there

Even when you tell yourself you don't really care

And though you know he wasn't going to stay

Your heart will still break as he walks away

Look into the mirror

what do you see

You think to yourself

Is that really me

It's not that you're ugly

Or fat or misshapen

Your mind just doesn't

Understand the equation

Time made you older

Your brain doesn't like it

But you're beautiful still

So don't try to fight it

Aging is hard

And so is believing

That there is still beauty

In the you that you're seeing

I'd do anything for you

Or so they say

But how far would they go

to make sure your ok

They're your parents

They love you

But they can hurt you too

You may hate them

In secret

Plotting to leave them

But someday you'll see

Just how much you need them

You could write poems about her beauty

But she wouldn't listen

Her heart had been hardened

By those who called her

Worthless

She saw him as a home

He saw her as a cheap motel

Only good enough for one night

He would leave her in the morning

I'd made it so the only place

I could see you

Was in my dreams

And now I can't even find you

There

I gave you what I thought

was love

And because of my inexperience

I was left alone

On the shore

With the others

Who would never be good enough

Love songs make it cheap

Movies make it worthless

But many feel as though

They don't deserve it

They say that they are loveless

They ask why they should care

They wonder if anybody notices

Them there

But in order to find love

You can't just stand around

You have to throw yourself

In the deep end

Even though you're scared you'll drown

I was alone until

You came along

And now that you're here

I'm scared that you might leave

Me alone

Again

I see him now

and wonder

If he

Knows

I would've gone

To the ends of the universe

For him

His smile used

To light up my world

But even

The brightest stars

Burn out

I never knew how much I missed it

The feeling of the ocean breeze on my face

Until I stood there on the edge with you

Thinking of you

Is the only way

I know to cope

With being

Without

You

My friend

Don't ever change

They will call you crazy

Let them

They are just jealous

of your confidence

They say all the lovely things

Have already been said

So i'll just lay here with you in silence

As we watch the stars

And i'll let you feel my love

Instead

"What do you think of me?" I asked

"You're beautiful" he said

But that's not what I wanted

I wanted him to describe the way I made him feel

Compare me to the galaxies

Tell me I was strong, that he thought I was brave

But all he could see was my body

Not the endless possibility inside

I don't want to look back on life

regretting all the chances

I didn't take

I must have done something right

After all I ended up with you

It's those late night thoughts

that hit me the hardest

Make me wonder

If my dreams will ever

Come true

But somewhere deep down

I know

I may not have all the answers

But that doesn't mean let go

Looking back now

I knew we wouldn't last

We burned too bright

For it to last forever

You were the missing piece

to someone else's puzzle

But I tried desperately

To fit you into the hole

In mine

In all the books

I've read

The girl

Is waiting

For a prince

Why can't she

Fall in love

With herself

Instead

Drag me away

From the city

With a sky full

Of stars

And i'll be

In paradise

I used to look at you

and see an angel

But now all I see

Is the devil that spawned

When your soul fell to earth

Are we angels or devils

Or something in between

Did we fall apart because of me

Or was it predestination

Nothing we could do?

It's funny that even now all I want is you

I have scars and I know they'll never fade

So why do I keep trying to do battle with a blade

People say what will be will be

Too afraid to be in charge of their own destiny

But if fate is irreversible, then what is my mind for

I promise to keep fighting, each and everyday

For the moment I give up is the moment I give up

Is the moment my last breath fades away

Laying under a sky full of stars

Their beauty only served

To remind me of you

All the best conversations

Happen when you've lost

A little sleep

And almost every sentence

Sounds so funny

That you can't help but

Die from laughter

It's always been you

It's always going to be you

I know you may not feel the same

But for you, I'd be happy being unhappy

As long as you don't hate me

I wanted to be the brightest star in the galaxy

The one everyone noticed

The one you couldn't help but love

But then I realized the brightest stars

Are the quickest to burn out

Leaving behind an empty hole

Not even scientists know how to fill

They say I'm a hopeless romantic

I guess what they say is true

All my love has been wasted

On loving a fool like you

I've watched him go from

A shy little boy

To a confident man

It's strange to see

The ones you love

Change before your eyes

If I had known then

Who he'd be now

I would have held him tight

Never let him go

He deserves the world

I don't know why it's so hard

To watch my friends get old

Oh god

It's the hardest

To get over

Someone

You never wanted

To let go

I wish I knew how

To say the words

To make someone

Fall in love

But the only way

I've found

Is to write them down

Where no one else

Can see

I don't know how to fix it

This inescapable mess

I want it to be over

But every time it ends

I just find another way

To screw myself

Over again

The ocean breeze

Was a siren song

Dragging me away

From the shore

Into the vast unknown

You thought that

you could break my heart

But the truth is

You didn't know me well enough

To find the cracks

That would make it fall apart

It's funny how someone can go

From the light of your life

To just another shadow

That haunts your dreams

Of what might have been

It's hard to write when you are happy

The inspiration only seems to come

When you have fallen to your knees

To pick up the broken pieces

Of your shattered soul

I never understood the saying

"Money can't buy happiness"

Until I went to a place

Where everyone had less

But were happier

Than anyone

I met

How did i know

I loved him?

Because when

It was over

Even though

He tore my heart

In two

I still wanted him

To be happy

I tried to hold in my feelings

But they condensed into

A flaming ball

So that when they finally

Escaped

It was a volcano

Of angry words

And tears

He broke my heart

And i wanted to die

But over time

I learned to

Love myself

I've taken my past

Locked it in a box

And dug a whole

So deep into

My heart

That no one else

Could ever find

The things i'd done

That had made me sad

Or angry or even happy

Because i needed to forget

Love

People believe it should be all consuming

Life changing, world shattering

But true love, is quiet, unexpected

Not jealous or proud

But understanding

And compassionate

It encourages your dreams,

And though the feelings may fade

The bond remains

Leaving you happy for the rest of your days

My mother always

Said ``don't change who you are"

She meant well i'm sure

But i've found that

Sometimes in order

To become

The truest version of yourself

You have to change the parts

That no longer belong

We all have that one person

That never fails to make us smile

But somewhere deep

Inside of us there's still

An empty feeling

As if even though

They make us smile

They don't really matter at all

I never know

When to leave

Or when to stay

I want to be loved

But don't

Know how to return

The feeling

I've had to let

So many go

Because

I was afraid

Of giving everything

Of me

For a feeling

I wasn't

Sure would

Last

After you left me

I swore to myself

That i had never loved you

But the reality was

You completely owned my heart

When you love someone

The feeling never leaves you

Even when they've moved on

And just seeing them

Stabs you through the heart

Because letting go is always the hardest part

I thought i

Let you go

A long time ago

But for the first time

I realized it was only yesterday

Too young to understand

But it sure felt nice

When he was holding my hand

Too young to realize

That nothing good

Comes out of lies

Too young to know

That sometimes it's better

To let them go

First love

Is supposed

To be beautiful

I tainted mine

With lies

What do you do

When your belief

In beauty dies?

Do you move on,

Let go,

Or rebuild your world,

Making sure to keep the ugly

Out?

Why can't she see

All the good

In me

Why must she choose

All the bad to focus on

Why do i have to live

With someone

Who hates me

As a child

Im sorry

Is all

You have to say

To make someone

Forgive you

Or push the pain

Away

But as you get older

Apologies mean less

And less

Until you wonder

If anyone is ever sorry

At all

Maybe i'm a fool

For loving you

Again

But maybe this time

It will never have to end

Maybe i'm a little crazy

The truth is

I didn't know

Just how much id

Miss you

When you finally

Let go

I don't ask for much

In the way of romance

Just a hand to hold

Eyes to get lost in

And a mind

With and endless

Trove of secrets to discover

Everytime i watch you go

Something inside me dies

But everytime you return

I hang my head and sigh

I know deep down i love you

But even as i say that

My heart is melancholy blue

For if you really love me

I wouldn't feel so alone

Even when i'm with you

Your name

Still echoes

In the depths

Of my soul

Even though

You're gone

I love you

But you shouldn't

Get too close

I have a habit

Of breaking

people

For so long

I blamed my broken heart

On everyone else

When the only

One to blame

Is myself

Seasons turn

Tides change

But i thought

That we could

Stay the same

Leaves fall

Breezes sigh

And we too

Fell apart

For even love

Must die

Don't give you heart

To the pretty boy

With the honeyed words

Give it to the one who makes

You smile

Even when you feel

Hopeless

Who makes you laugh

When on the verge of

Tears

And only makes you cry from joy

Never from heartbreak

Love is meant to be felt

Not always in joy

But also in the times

When your heart aches

From missing it so

But knowing it's never

Truly out of reach

I want you so badly

But i'm afraid that us

Together

Would lead to both of us

Falling apart

You and i

are soulmates

See?

But there

Is always

Something

Between you

And me

I know deep down

I should

Let it go

But i hold out

Hope that we

Will be forever

I'd stopped

Believing in

Love

And then you

showed up

And proved

It did

Exist

He's been in my life

So long

That i don't

Know what

Life

Is like without

him

You've inspired

so many

Of my

Poems

And you don't

Even know it

Our love

Was a sinking ship

But somehow

I was the only one

To drown

I wasn't sure how i felt

Until it

Was too late

To have a chance

When I met you

I was so young

scared of love

and what it does

I'm older now

and wish I knew

that I'd love you more

the more we grew

I'm scared to leave

don't want to go

but it's time to move on

let my world grow

I'm scared

of leaving

because I'm

scared to lose

everything

that makes me

feel safe

Her eyes

were like

the ocean

before a storm

a calm gray

with an undercurrent

of the chaos to come

I miss you

But i can

Live without

You

I love you

And i wish you knew

How much

But right now

I have to make it on my own

I don't want to lose you

But i'll learn to let you go

Even if it breaks me

Apart

Maybe we are like peter and wendy

You won't grow up and i won't stay young

But i love you against all the impossible odds

The worst thing

A person could do

Is breaks a heart

Hoping

No one else

Can put it back

Together

I felt more feelings about you

Than anyone else

But you gave me no choice

But to try and move on

I tried to blame him

For never

Seeing my love

But if i never showed

It

Then whose fault is it really?

How do you know if he's the one

It's not as if he placed the moon

And hung the sun

He's just a boy

Not yet a man

But you'd be so happy

If you could hold his hand

It's crazy that you fell so fast

But he's just so cute and he makes you laugh

You dont know why don't know how

You may not end up working out

But he's all you care about right now

You told me i was beautiful

And for once

I started to believe it

I used to write

Only when i was sad

Emotions pouring out of

Me like a waterfall

I didn't know

What to do with it

But now i'll try writing when

Im happy

All because of you

He broke my heart

Left me alone

Without a reason

But then came back to tell me

It was my fault

For not letting him

Love me

I look at you

And see

Everything

That once

Was

And it pains me

To see just

How much

Has changed

I love him

More than anyone

But one

And it scares me

I'll never let that one go

I wish i could

Look at him

Without seeing

The past present and

Future all at once

Im so damn tired

Of being ignored

By someone

Who loved me once

Because im no longer

What they want

I see the road not taken

And i want to run down

It

But don't know

If he'll be waiting

At the end

I can't look at you

Without seeing

All the

Memories

And it makes

I want to

Cry

I miss him in a way

Thats different

From everyone

Else

I've loved

Before

But somehow

It hurts

Less

I'm sick

Of being

Everyones

Emotional

Support

Only to

Be

Left alone

When im

The

One

Who

Hurts

your scent

was in the wind

today

it didn't hurt

like i thought it

would

instead it felt

like a sign

that someday

you'd come home

for good

it's an ache

an empty promise

a love gone too soon

i want to fight it

but my bones are tired

i can no longer hold up

the weight of loving

i want to

run into battle

to turn the tide

to keep him close

to stay at his side

but life said no

at least for now

who knows what will happen

i just wish i did

i'm begging

please don't go

watching as he

crumbles

before my eyes

is that the truth

is he really falling apart

or is it my tears

and my

screams

making him disappear

sometimes

the person

you'd take a

bullet for

is the one holding the gun

and sometimes

the one you want to reach for

when your world is collapsing

is the reason it's falling apart

but sometimes you just have

more love for someone

than the universe knows

what to do with

i thought

i'd felt heartbreak

before

but this hurts

a million times

Worse

you said

i wasn't listening

you were right

i was trying to drown out

the sound of my breaking

heart

my best writing

comes from pain

so i guess i should thank you

for inspiring me

again

how am i

expected to move on

when you are all

i want

even after you

broke me

to make yourself

feel better

if you called

right now

i'd come running

forever putting

how i feel

over how

i should hate you

it's not my fault

you are broken

but it still feels

like my

responsibility

to fix

you

all i wanted

from the start

was someone to love

who wouldn't break my heart

i should've left when it started to hurt

but i stayed, convinced love would win

once again my heart was wrong.

love isn't enough to fix our

broken parts

yet i still hold out hope

because my heart just won't

let you go

our souls are broken

in the same places

burnt and bruised

from others damage

but it's those

imperfections

that bring our

two halves

into one

perfect

whole

he was all i wanted

but he left just the same

you'd think after the last times

i would have made a change

i'm always my own downfall

it's really such a shame

they claim they love me

need me

but leave instead of stay

what are you supposed to do

feeling broken feeling used

all i wanted was love

once again i lost it

was it all me

i'll never know

but i just feel so forgotten

why am i always the runner up

the one whose heart gets broken

i thought this time was different

but it's always just the same.

i hate the people who break my heart

but i run to them anyway

i'm hurting

bending breaking

lost in the pain of

my own making

i love you

i hate you

can't live without you

all i want is

to move on

shake this hold

you have on me

it's been years

but i can't let go

i know you've moved on

and it hurts to see

why can't these feelings

set me free

when the world goes quiet my head gets loud.

the pills don't work to keep the volume down.

it's taking all i've got to keep them from getting the better of me.

i just need something to set me free

I'm dying here

and no one seems to care

they want me to stay

but it's time for me to go

I just want to be happy

and I'll be happier

at home

break my own heart easy

never knowing what to say

let them love my body freely

don't even make them pay

all i want is to feel special

and i end up feeling used

what's the point of loving

if they end up leaving too

i can't delete them

your pictures off my phone

i see you smiling happy

remember how you looked at me

i wanted to love you

you didn't give me that chance

and now i want to hate you

but these photos are all

that i have

it's getting bad again

the demons in my head seem relentless

i can't drown out the screaming

i beg to turn the volume down

but only you could drown them out

and now you're gone

and they keep getting louder

won't shut up or go to sleep

and i'm restless

why did you abandon me

i fall in love too easy

and i knew this from the start

you said you wouldn't run

but then you disappeared

i told you all my problems

you said you'd stick around

now i'm left alone

losing sleep because I slept best

next to you.

i didn't have you long

but still i'm afraid

of the scars i'm sure are there

I break everything i touch

nothing ever lasts.

i hope that you move on

find a person good for you

I know now im too poisonous

to ever see things through.